What There Is, As It Is

The Epigrammatic Poems of Ludwig Feuerbach

Martin Wasserman

508 West 26th Street KEARNEY, NE 68848
402-819-3224
info@medialiteraryexcellence.com

INTRODUCTION

Ida Overbeck, one of Friedrich Nietzsche's closest friends, claimed that in a conversation she had with him, the philosopher declared that the strongest influence on his literary style whether it be the longer pieces or the very short ones, like the epigrams was the work of Ludwig Feuerbach. In his book Love, Death, and Revolution in Central Europe, Peter Caldwell asserted that of all the mid-nineteenth century German social philosophers, Feuerbach was the only one who actually had a strong sense of humor. Taking into account both the fact that Nietzsche had such great admiration for one of his predecessors and the knowledge that a German philosopher could actually be called "witty," I knew that I just had to engage in a project which dealt with the writings of Ludwig Feuerbach.

After careful consideration I chose to make my specific undertaking the translations of some of Feuerbach's epigrammatic poems. I made this decision because, as far as I could determine, this type of task had not been attempted in over thirty-five years. Furthermore, I believed that the last translation, as good as it was, certainly left room for a different approach to Feuerbach's playful verse. With this thought in mind, my new strategy for translating the epigrams was to recognize them as being part of everyday speech and conversation; then to come as close as I possibly could to making a proper English translation which would allow the reader to appreciate not only the content of Feuerbach's remarks but also the way in which he articulated these remarks through the use of epigrammatic verse. (Please note that towards the end of this introductory section there will be more said on the matter of "a proper English translation.")

Ludwig Feuerbach was born on July 28, 1804 in Landshut, Bavaria, a state in southern Germany. After a relatively uneventful childhood and adolescence, he started college at the University of Heidelberg with the intention of becoming a theologian, but just weeks after arriving the restless Feuerbach decided to transfer to the University of Berlin where he hoped to complete his course work. However, once matriculated at this new and larger college, he became intrigued by the ideas of Georg Wilhelm Hegel and soon began to study philosophy in earnest. Feuerbach completed his education at the University of Erlangen, the result of still another transfer on his part, and it was here, in 1828, that he received his doctorate of philosophy.

Two years later Feuerbach wrote and published his first book entitled Thoughts on Death and Immortality. In this work, Feuerbach refuted the notion of personal immortality and, instead, advanced the belief that immortality was nothing more than a reabsorption back into nature. Even though this idea, in part, kept him from a future academic career, it did, however, set the stage for his more influential writings like The Essence of Christianity. This work, published in 1841, looked at religion as a form of self-deception. Feuerbach argued that persons unconsciously project their best qualities into an imaginary external and eternal being whom they call "God." Feuerbach then went on to claim that people with common sense would be well-advised to use science and technology, instead of relying upon supernatural entities, to fulfill all their worldly goals and desires.

Ludwig Feuerbach's most important work, Lectures on the Essence of Religion, published ten years later (in 1851), consisted of a series of scholarly talks which the philosopher periodically gave to both academics and the general public. In this work, Feuerbach expounded on the themes he first put forth in The Essence of Christianity by arguing even more vigorously for the diminished role of religion, along with a concomitant strengthening of science, to explain all of life's varied and unusual experiences.

With his scholarly background in the areas of religion, philosophy, and science, Feuerbach was uniquely qualified to analyze, evaluate, and draw conclusions when it came to any single theological issue of consequence. However, Feuerbach's intentions were much broader. Having set his focus on an individual's relationship to the metaphysical world, Feuerbach devoted his adult years to recasting religion in general and Christianity in particular from an essentially humanistic perspective.

There are two other factors as well which helped Feuerbach earn a great deal of respect from both his philosophy colleagues and the lay readers of his books. First, his anthropological interest in studying "the absolute and the exalted" compelled Feuerbach to bring these very abstract and complex subjects back down to a personal level where they had a much better chance of influencing real people in their everyday lives. Second, with his focus directed towards reason, cooperation, and mutual understanding, Feuerbach was determined to show that a relationship between the self and others (or as he called it, "I and Thou") is more essential and rewarding than any kind of faith-based desire for a supernatural communion.

Feuerbach's groundbreaking work, over time, was able to influence other important social philosophers and theologians such as Karl Marx, Martin Buber, and Karl Barth. By minimizing religion and, instead, embracing material and worldly factors, Feuerbach consistently engaged in serious philosophical investigations which, afterwards, were often used by him to explain the human condition. Furthermore, because of his relentless questioning of established societal values, Feuerbach was able to construct a basic sociological foundation for the later revolutionary work of Marx and Engels.

Ludwig Feuerbach died from natural causes on September 13, 1872 in Nuremberg. Besides each of the major book titles which have already been mentioned in this "Introduction," Feuerbach wrote three other important and influential works which also should be noted. In the order of their publication dates, the titles of these books are Toward a Critique of Hegelian Philosophy (1839), Principles and Philosophy of the Future (1843), and The Question of Immortality from the Standpoint of Anthropology (1846).

An epigrammatic poem is a short, pithy, and hopefully clever piece of verse which, as a rule, expresses a single thought or observation. I mention this almost universally accepted definition of the epigram because there is one major difference between an epigrammatic poem written in German and one that is composed in English. The standard for any piece of good poetry in English, including the epigram, is that the words and lines flow in some type of metrical pattern, whether that pattern be iambic pentameter, iambic tetrameter, or, for that matter, any other kind of established metrical form. However, when epigrammatic verse is written in German, the standard strived for is not that of being metrical but, rather, how close a piece of verse can come to sounding like ordinary speech or conversation. Walter Kaufmann, the eminent translator and essayist, has stressed this fact. He bluntly stated that when it comes to doing translation work on epigrammatic poems in German, those persons "who consider it their job to transpose all they touch into whatever they consider poetic or the peculiar verse idiom of the day…miss the point that most German epigrammatists have always tried to stay extremely close to the spoken language."

Not wanting to fall into any sort of metrical or lyrical trap, I heeded Kaufmann's advice when I was doing my translations of Feuerbach's epigrammatic verse. I envisioned, with each piece I was working on, that the poem itself actually represented a particular set of verbal remarks which Feuerbach wished to personally deliver to any English reader who was desirous to hear what he had to say. The reader then, on each page that he or she was looking at, would be thrust into the dual roles of both reader and listener; but it was Feuerbach who would be shaping their relationship of course, with the aid of English translations by being both the author and speaker who initially put forward all those strong verbal assertions which are recorded on each page.

WHAT THERE IS,
AS IT IS

-"I think I summed up my attitude to philosophy
when I said: philosophy ought really to be
written only as a poetic composition."-

Ludwig Wittgenstein

Prevent a tree from expressing itself
in leaves, flowers, or fruit,
and it will wither away; prevent love
from expressing itself, and it will be
choked
by its own vitality.
—

"Faith moves mountains!"
If by this we mean
that faith does not solve
difficult problems
but merely pushes them aside,
then certainly!

———

The reality
of a hereafter
helps me about as much
as the thought
of a future Sunday roast
on Monday,
when I'm hungry
only for a paycheck.

—

Good books
those that give us
something to think about
are written in a foreign language;
it is only
by reading them
that we are able
to translate the text
into our mother tongue.
———

What there is, as it is
truth expressed truly
often appears superficial;
while, strangely,
what there is,
as it is not
truth expressed backwards
is the one truth
that resonates deeply
with all its eager proponents.

—

Death is acceptable
if it arrives
at the proper time,
but if it arrives
too early
it is a burdensome guest.
It's no wonder, then,
that even the most cherished visitor
is simply a pain
if he arrives
earlier
than expected.

—

To be in the body
means
to be in the world;
so much skin
with so many pores,
so many bare spots!
Sometimes it seems
that the body
is nothing more
than a porous self.

—

There are those
who have overloaded their stomachs
with morals;
then afterwards,
for dessert,
they still insist
on serving up God.

—

If you wish to uncover
the treasures of your homeland,
you must walk away
from them; similarly,
persons must first become
detached from their egos
if they wish to know their
own true value.

—

The deepest secrets of life
can be found
in the simplest natural things.
If you tell me what you eat,
I'll tell you who you are
for, in the end,
you are what you eat.

—

What else is love
but an eternity
of pain and joy
in one single breath?

———

Once again
the clowns have taken over
the contemporary stage,
while sorrow,
with little fanfare,
quietly keeps
the home fires burning.
——

You do not frighten us
for we already know
from history
that many an ass
lies hidden
beneath a lion's skin.

—

The true qualities
of a person
show themselves
only when it is time
for them to be shown;
only at that juncture
when they are ready
to be put
into necessary action.

—

Life
is the springtime
of our thoughts, but sometimes it seems
that when we are writing about life
it is already
late autumn.

—

What is the afterlife?
Only a paraphrase
of this life;
whoever understands
the original language needs
no translation.
—

Do not grieve
over your mistakes!
Errors are just
unhappy virtues
virtues
that lack the opportunity
to show themselves as being
themselves.

—

The text of our life
when we reminisce
seems far too often,
and in far too
many ways,
to be lifted
from the libretto
of a really bad opera.

———

Nobody
is destined for happiness
but all are destined for life,
seeing that somehow we're
all participating in it.
Love, however, always
and above all else
gives each specific life
its most unforgettable pleasures
while, at the same time,
staging its most daunting calamities.
—

Food
that we ourselves grow
tastes better perhaps
not because
it really is better God forbid!
but only because we
ourselves
have cultivated it.

———

Whoever
grasps evil by its roots
is digging deeply;
indeed, if you just rip
off some branches,
you really don't know
the tree.

—

We link
the highest objects of thought
with the most common
needs and phenomena,
so that even in the intestines
of animals one still can
conceive of spiritual
food in need of
worldly speculation.

———

It is not to be denied,
he displays overwhelming passion;
but is he now ready to sizzle on a bed
of red-hot promises?

———

A bible
that is written
in a particular language
cannot be
the divine Word.

—

Those who wish to find
that one pure thing in life
are like animals on a barren heath
driven round and round by crazed spirits;
while right there,
straight in front of them,
is that one pure bountiful,
beautiful grazing ground
just waiting
for their arrival.

—

What is the surest sign
that a religion
no longer possesses
inner vitality?
The answer is simple:
when the wealthy of this world
have to stretch out their
arms in order
to lift churchgoers
back on their feet.

—

Truth does not give you
the rust of old fables; it consoles you
with an authentic humanity which exists
because you are existing,
both kindly and wisely.
—

Once I believed
Thinking to be the purpose
of life, but now I
know that life
is the purpose of thinking.
—

Once you are nothing,
are No-Thing,
the eternity behind you lies
ahead of you, too;
awareness of this in the here
and now can wash your eyes,
give you light,
and even restore bright features.
—

What we suffer here
will never be rectified
in heaven,
for only the goodness
of today heals the pain
of tomorrow.

———

Life is not tolerant
since nature plays
no practical jokes;
and certainly
the end is not a hollow jest
for death,
no matter what else it may be,
is no comedian.

—

The pain of love means
that the loving picture
which is in your imagination is not
in reality.

—

Surely, our lover, if he desires it,
has the opportunity
to burn his selfishness, like tinder,
in time's everlasting
fire of intimacy.
———

You can piece together old rags
as much as you want, but you will never come up
with a durable coat.

—

Whoever needs to unravel
life's great mysteries
would be well-advised to first
withdraw into a library;
for, as any clever book detective knows,
this is truth's wondrous
"recovery and discovery" zone.

—

The genuine writer cannot be a
coward, for he does not fear
self-sacrifice; instead,
he condenses and compresses
the entire energy
of his soul into the
incandescent lens
of his writings.

—

If you want to know what it is to be human,
find out what an individual hates;
you see, hate is always a better indicator of the
human psyche than love.
—

The hereafter is beautiful only in a dream,
not as a reality unto itself; it looks good to us
but only from a distance.

—

Past time is always beautiful time
when it brings light to the
dullness of memory.

—

If there is life after death, then, logically,
that means there cannot also
be its converse: life before death.

—

Time exists only on that boundary
which lies between you
and your very next
thought.

—

The more our relationship
with good books increases,
the smaller becomes
that circle of people whose
company we truly enjoy.

—

The most interesting thing
about writing
is not that one becomes
known to the world but, rather,
it's through writing
that one can get to know the world
although not necessarily
from its best side.

—

The eternal is that whose
end is also my end.

—

You ask whether one day
I will be unhappy with you
this I cannot know;
but what I do know
is that today my joy is truly a
genuine joy
only when I'm right
beside you.

—

The faults of individuals should
Routinely be viewed
as just their very special
virtues incognito.

—

When
there is no "thou,"
there is no "I."

—

Question: Do you know why Adam bit the apple?
Response: Simply to grant a favor to theology.

—

Just think of this!
In most languages
"belief" is considered masculine
but dear "reason"
that's only the little woman
struggling to be heard.
—

"Atheism" is nothing more
than "pantheism"
in reverse.
—

The truth of the matter
is that whatever life brings it can
also take away;
certainly, during our lifetimes
we will have the opportunity to
hear from both guilt and
reconciliation on this
particular
subject.

—

Nature provides no response
to the questions
and sorrows of man;
uncompromisingly, it simply
allows the individual,
once again,
to fall back upon
himself.

———

Recollection alone is the true
realm of the dead; it alone
is the special land
of time's departed
souls.

———

The "thou" between a loving man
and woman has quite an
appealing sound to it when compared to the
monotonous tones found
in most everyday human
relationships.

—

What is pseudolove?
Surely the supposed unity
between thought and being, when
Being is valued just as a woman and
Thought, just as a man.

—

Dogma,
no matter where it's found,
must be judged as
nothing else but the expressed
prohibition of thinking.

———

Man, first, unconsciously
and involuntarily
created God in his own image;
then afterwards, religion, consciously
and voluntarily, hoped for a recreated man
quite similar to that divine being
it had once brought forth.
Of course, this is the kind of
hopeful wish that, unceremoniously,
should now be referred to
as "wishful thinking."

—

POSTSCRIPT

Martin Wasserman, the translator of this work, is a Professor Emeritus at SUNY Adirondack, a college in the State University of New York system, where he taught for thirty-six years. During his career he published over thirty journal articles and three books. One of those works, *Kafka Kaleidoscope*, was chosen as a "Best Book" by the Small Press Review in 1999. Professor Wasserman's two most recent works are an original piece called *Busy Searching for Light: Some Modern English Tanka* and a translation entitled: *Kafka, Rilke, Nadel: Three German Writers Pulling Me Toward the East.*

It should be noted that the one phrase which is most frequently associated with Feuerbach "you are what you eat" does not have the same meaning today as it did when it first appeared in Feuerbach's powerful essay, "Concerning Spiritualism and Materialism." Whereas we use this phrase today as a nutritional guideline to promote healthy eating habits, Feuerbach intended it to be a call to the masses to rebel against all those rigid and harmful class distinctions in Western European life whose sole purpose was to "keep people in their place."

It should also be noted that my primary source for almost all of Feuerbach's epigrammatic poems was *Frühe Schriften, Kritiken und Reflexionen*, 18281834 (in English, *Early Writings, Criticisms, and Reflections*, 1828-1834).